EDUCATI
DEMOCRACY

EDUCATION AND DEMOCRACY

Against the Educational Establishment

Anthony O'Hear

**The Claridge Press
London**

First published in Great Britain 1991

by The Claridge Press
6 Linden Gardens
London W2 4ES
and Box 420
Lexington
Georgia 30648

Typeset by
JCL
Frome
and printed by
Short Run Press
Exeter, Devon

ISBN 1-870626-91-5

O'Hear, Anthony: *Education & Democracy: Against the Educational Establishment*

1. Politics
2. Education

EDUCATION AND DEMOCRACY

Against the Educational Establishment

Education cannot be democratic. In a democratic society, therefore, the role and organisation of education are extremely problematic affairs.

Education cannot be democratic because educating involves imparting to a pupil something which he has yet to acquire. The imparting has to be done by someone who possesses what the pupil lacks. The transaction is therefore inevitably between unequals. The value of the transaction cannot be known to the pupil in advance. Since it will result in a change in the knowledge, wisdom and values of the pupil, he cannot truly assess what the worth of that change will be for him. Others, more experienced than he, must make that judgement. Education, then, is irretrievably authoritarian and paternalist.

A Crisis in Education

That there is a crisis in British education is widely accepted outside the educational establishment, and widely accepted inside it by those who are prepared to be honest. The Conservative government responded to the crisis by a number of measures, culminating in the Educational Reform Act of 1988. The Labour party is making the crisis in education a key focus of its campaign for the next election. I would not be surprised if it does quite well with the campaign, because users of the education service are well aware of its inadequacies and many are sceptical of the efficacy of the Reform Act. I share this scepticism, but I am also doubtful that the Labour Party will do any better.

The Education Reform Act has as its centre piece the centralisation of the curriculum and examinations in the hands of the government. Schools are being given some degree of managerial autonomy, which is no doubt a good thing, and parents more choice than they had over the schools to which they may send their children. But these liberalising measures will mean little in the context of the control now vested in the Secretary of State over what is taught in schools. In fact, of course,it will not be the Secretary of State whose baleful influence will permeate the educational system. The bearer of that office is but a transitory Gastarbeiter in the realms of Scholesia. Real control in that state-within-a-state is in the hands of its permanent and tenured citizens, the officials of the Department of Education and Science, Her Majesty's Inspectors, Local Authority Advisors, trainers of teachers in University and College Departments of Education and members of the non-accountable quangoes such as the National Curriculum Council and the Schools Examination and Assessment Council.

As shown in a report in *The Daily Mail* (13.11.90) there are now nearly 400,000 non-teachers employed by the DES and Local Education Authorities, about the same total as that of classroom teachers. Up to one-third of these non-teachers are in educational administration. Over the last year, while the number of teachers has dropped by over 5,000, the number of non-teachers has gone up by 2,500. Even more significantly, the number of teachers employed by Educational Authorities who are not actually teaching has gone up in the last ten years from 3.7% to 7.7% of the total teaching force. David Hart, of the Association of Head Teachers, estimates that there are 20,000 education advisors in Local Authorities, at a cost of £500 million per year. All this, of course, is in contrast to the independent sector, which runs on a minimum of bureaucracy; and all this is in a period of declining pupil numbers and alleged teacher shortages.

It is my view that the educational bureaucracy should be dismantled. This proposal will, of course, be fought tooth and nail, by those with a vested interest in opposing it. But it is vital that we do attack the bureaucracy, because among the citizens of Scholesia, there is an orthodoxy which militates against any true practice of education. It is an orthodoxy which may be inevitable in a democracy, because it arises from the demand to make education democratic — something it can never be. But it is an orthodoxy to which the Education Reform Act has given unprecedented power through the National Curriculum and ministerial control of examinations.

The Labour Party, meanwhile, watches the discomfiture of the government with not a little *Schadenfreude*. In a recent advertisement it highlighted the facts that British teenagers are, on average, two years behind their German counterparts in mathematics, that a survey in 1987 showed that 44% of the population cannot read a fire safety notice, that teachers are leaving the profession faster than they can be recruited. The Labour Party, then, is happy enough to take note of the symptoms of our educational crisis, the appalling standards of reading, writing, numeracy and behaviour found in so many of our schools, the fact that even Her Majesty's Inspectors find that a third of all lessons are less than satisfactory, that two million of our children get a raw deal from state schools, that maths teaching in a quarter of primary schools is poor and that two-thirds of all primary school science lessons are sub-standard, and so on and so forth. But, from the outside, one may be forgiven for doubting that the Labour Party has the solution in its hands.

The Labour Party advocates more nursery education, more access to education, more power to local authorities, more pay for teachers, when what is actually needed is less of what goes under the name of education, less access to inappropriate forms of education, less power to local authorities and a thorough review of a teaching profession which, for twenty years or more, has been indoctrinated in the anti-educational ideas that the ruling classes of Scholesia have propagated from their positions of power and authority. The Labour Party is also proposing a central Educational Standards Council, with power to inspect independent as well as maintained schools, when what is needed is less centralisation and more diversity in education, something the Party is even now unwilling to

countenance, apparently insisting still on single curricula and examinations for all pupils.

Nor, indeed, is there any evidence that our educational crisis
is due to lack of resources. Not only has spending per child increased
by 42% in real terms since 1979, but we spend a higher proportion
of our Gross National Product on education than either Germany or
Japan, whose standards are far higher than ours. By contrast the
USA, which regularly outspends other countries on education, also
regularly fails disastrously on international education comparisons.
What counts is not how much a country spends on education *in toto*,
but how usefully the money is deployed.

The Inspectorate

Let us look at the situation in a little more detail, beginning with Her
Majesty's Inspectors, from whose reports many of the bleak find-
ings recounted in the previous section are taken. These reports give
the impression that in the Inspectorate we have a body of detached,
impartial observers, carefully and beadily overseeing standards on
behalf of the rest of us. But this impression is very far from the truth.
Far from being detached from educational trends and politics, the
Inspectors are key players in the game. While deploring manifest
failure, in their own publications and reports they consistently
advocate the very policies which have put education in its present
state.

Over the past decade they have criticised secondary schools
explicitly for not developing multi-ethnic programmes and implic-
itly for failing to make systematic provision for the treatment of
issues connected with equal opportunities, as they put it in the
inimitable jargon of ed-speak. They have complained about 'teacher-
dominated' lessons in English and insisted that non-standard (that is,
often ungrammatical) English be left unrebuked. The study of
poetry is seen as a spring-board for pupils' own emoting, on the
grounds that 'all writing connected with the experience of poetry is
creative'. In Music from 5-16 the teaching of pop songs is required.

On History, schools are criticised for relying on secondary sources (i.e. text books) which allow children to learn 'historical facts', but which do not foster historical skills (those of empathy, evaluation of evidence, information-finding and rest, whose proper grasp eludes, in fact, all but the most knowledgeable historians).

The Inspectors complain about mathematics in primary schools, as well they might. But their own examples of good practice are nearly all of measuring, cutting, making, ranking and counting things: an approach to mathematics likely to lead to the idea that it is an empirical science, based on the observation of material things, rather than an abstract, theoretical discipline whose strength and applicability is precisely that it is not itself a practical matter.

In primary school science, the emphasis is on 'action knowledge' and encouraging the chatter of pupils, while a pamphlet on classics in independent schools speaks of a 'desirable move away from some of the values and methods traditionally associated with classical language teaching'. The Inspectorate advocates what it calls those aspects of the curriculum which fall between subject boundaries, such as environmental, political and social education, with all the scope that implies for indoctrination on the part of teachers and tendentiousness on the part of pupils. Its publications abound with the standard ritual denunciation of 'passive' learning, that is learning in which the teacher assumes full authority, and it employs the vacuous jargon of 'transferable skills'. Furthermore, it insists that teaching must match the existing interest and experience of the pupils, an absurd contention when pupils' existing interest and experience are by definition uneducated.

Ludicrously, but quite predictably, in 1990 the Inspectorate criticised Hyland House School, a private Seventh Day Adventist school in Waltham Forest with an all-black clientele, for lack of 'multi-cultural resources'. The Inspectors also found 'an over-emphasis on English', and in mathematics of 'an over-emphasis on the use of text-books and arithmetical work copied from the black-board' at the expense, apparently, of the use of calculators. These negative comments were made of a school of 90 pupils and a waiting list of 150, to which parents are prepared to pay £340 per term to ensure that their children are exposed to spelling and grammar and where the pupils attain what even the Inspectors admit are satisfactory standards in reading, and 'a fairly secure grasp of number and of basic arithmetical processes'.

Not surprisingly in view of all these opinions, the Inspectorate has endorsed the GCSE, commending the move in that examination away from writing towards practical, oral and investigative work. In other words, the Inspectors lend their support to the sentimental and ultimately pernicious view of education as play and discovery, rather than the disciplined entry into serious, already existing forms of civilised life.

The GCSE

Before its introduction in 1988 and the consequent demise of GCE 'O' levels, the GCSE was promoted as an examination suitable for all pupils at the age of 16. It was conceived and administered by what is now the Schools Examination and Assessment Council under explicit guidance from the DES. The Secondary Examinations Council, as it was originally called, was set up in 1983 'to advise the Secretaries of State on how the school examinations and assessment system can best serve the needs of the education service and its client'. As well as overseeing the GCSE, the Council is charged with monitoring other courses which are offered to pupils during their years of compulsory schooling. Clearly, then, in the GCSE, if anywhere, we will find the 'official view' of education that permeates the educational establishment in this country. And indeed we do, right from the very premise on which it is based, namely that there ought to be one single examination for all pupils after eleven years of schooling. To a Martian, or even to a visitor from Germany or Japan, this might seem a preposterous proposition, but then they have not been softened up for it by the creation of comprehensive schools and the consequent erasure of distinctions of ability in education even at the secondary level.

Prior to 1973, the majority of pupils left school with no academic qualification. Many pupils were in schools with academic pretensions. The policies of raising the school leaving age and making the education system comprehensive were egalitarian in inspiration, intended to play down differences in pupils — differences in ability, motivation and interest. The logical consequence of having all pupils in the same school for longer periods is to have them all sitting the same examination. And so the GCSE was conceived, and eventually born, under a Conservative administration, and a Secretary of State who was for the first time vested with direct control over school examinations.

It is hard to see how anybody other than a group of dogmatic egalitarians, cosily insulated from the real world, could ever have imagined that a satisfactory single examination could be devised for all pupils in all schools after 11 years of compulsory schooling. Hence the confusing plethora of grades given in the GCSE, the differences of style of examination permitted within it, and the differences of target offered to different candidates.

But beneath all this confusion, the GCSE as a whole presages a decline in academic standards. Why else do some independent schools spend the first term of the sixth form doing what was formerly O-level work in physics and chemistry? Why else is there talk of A-level science syllabuses being cut by 15 per cent? Why else are university vice-chancellors talking of the need for changes in university courses when the first GCSE-education students begin to come through? Why else do only 12% of biology teachers believe that the GCSE has improved 'study skills' (a significant finding, in view of the unlikely but popular claim that content-free courses and examinations enhance 'study skills')?

A decline in academic standards is inevitable, given the ideology and practice of the GCSE: an insistence that subjects be made relevant to pupils' existing interests (rather than giving them new and better interests), large tracts of time-consuming, but not necessarily taxing, project work (supervised how?), examinations set and assessed within schools (evaluated how and by whom?), the profligacy with which high grades have been awarded in GCSE (25 per cent more high grades in key subjects than with O-level) and a substitution of ill-defined skills for substantive curricular content as the goal of schooling.

On the inflation of standards brought about by the GCSE, some heads of independent schools are now showing embarrassment at the high percentage of A grades their pupils are achieving in the GCSE: 90% or more in many cases. They know that their pupils are not that good. And if the GCSE is supposed to do away with the divisiveness and low standing of the CSE, on this count too, it is a failure. Widespread among employers there is now a belief that anything less than a C grade at GCSE is to all intents and purposes worthless.

It was rumoured that when Kenneth Baker was Secretary of State for Education, the government hoped to pull back what was being lost through the GCSE by means of the national curriculum. Mr Baker was clearly disturbed by the fact that pupils could take GCSE history by concentrating on topics such as one's local church and oral history without ever being acquainted with what he liked to call the broad narrative flow of British (and, I would add, European) history. To a limited extent, but only after direct ministerial interference and against the curriculum working party's original advice, the national curriculum for History does address this worry, just as the national curriculum for English does attempt to do similar things for English, and the Geography working party is attempting to rebut the GCSE view of Geography as primarily political. But it would be unwise to rest much faith in the National Curriculum Council (or indeed in the effectiveness of Secretaries of State for Education). The National Curriculum Council has been in the forefront of the assault on A-levels, the one area of our school education system where standards have remained fairly high and reasonably academic. It is, as yet, unclear how far Secretaries of State will be able to preserve A-levels against an assault to which the whole of the educational establishment and the Labour Party seem committed.

The National Curriculum Council

In April 1990, the National Curriculum Council proposed that six 'core' skills, together with work experience, be incorporated into all A-level study programmes (and Mr John MacGregor, the then Secretary of State for Education, instead of condemning such claptrap out of hand, responded by asking the Schools Examination and Assessment Council to advise how this could be done). According to the Curriculum Council 'there is still too wide a gap between education and training' and employers want the gap closed in the way they propose. Now, while employers clearly want employable people who can read and write and calculate, it is not obvious that this means they want an education based on the concept of core skills, rather than one based on traditional subjects taught well and in depth and for their own sake.

On a number of occasions recently I have heard of highly placed employers in computing asking for well-rounded graduates in philosophy and the humanities rather than for people trained specifically in information technology or computing science. Even if employers' representatives were misguidedly to demand that educators see themselves primarily as trainers of a workforce, the proper response should be to reassert the distinction between education and training and not, as the National Curriculum Council does, explicitly to advocate its eradication.

Education involves the transmission to individuals of what is valuable in itself: knowledge of mathematics, the natural world, the humanities, our cultural and historical heritage. Education gives the educated man what he would otherwise lack and what mere training cannot supply: the wherewithal to make reasoned judgments about the worth of various ends and goals, as well as entry into a number of activities worth pursuing for their own sake and not as means to some other end. A concern for education therefore distinguishes a civilised people from one which sees individuals simply as elements in a comprehensive plan.

Even in a civilised society, training is necessary; but it should concern means not ends. Education can only be corrupted if it is seen in terms of the contribution it might make to the training of a workforce. But this is exactly what the National Curriculum Council does. In speaking of the six core skills of post-16 education ("communication, problem-solving, personal skills, numeracy, information technology and modern language competence") the Council is indifferent to the value or content of what is taught, seeing it only in terms of how it might contribute to its skills programme. In addition to teaching their subjects, teachers are expected by the Council to mark and profile their pupils in these supposed skills, awarding grades which will affect the outcome of their A-levels.

As I and many others have frequently pointed out, without ever getting a satisfactory answer, an entirely bogus notion of skill is being employed here. Solving problems, communicating and organising one's work are entirely different matters in the study of physics from what they are in the study of literature. Music is different yet again, and so on for all the subjects. The skills involved in each study are not something extra which can be detached and transferred indiscriminately to other areas. How, for example, do musical skills help the mathematician or historical skills the physicist? A skill in communicating through dance or movement is unlikely to help a philosopher to expound Wittgenstein, nor is an ability to solve problems in higher mathematics of any obvious relevance to solving the problem of buying a railway ticket from a machine or that of changing a car tyre in the dark.

The other three core skills are those of numeracy, modern languages and information technology. Providing that education before the age of 16 had been satisfactory, there is no good reason why those doing serious A-level work should be burdened with any of this, where it is not already an integral part of what they are studying. 'O'-level mathematics and language teaching used to be quite enough for non-specialists, and information technology is of negligible educational value, compared to the reading of Homer or the proper study of sience.

No teacher with a real passion for his subject would analyze his work in the hollow jargon of skills, and this alone casts doubts on the National Curriculum Council's understanding of what education is. In advocating breadth of study, the Council is in effect preventing those who could and would excel in some particular field from doing so. But this is hardly surprising given the composition of the Council and its roots in the educational establishment, an establishment which sees education as a means of global social engineering rather than as an end to be pursued for its own sake.

The Schools Assessment and Examination Council

After this softening up by the National Curriculum Council, the Schools Assessment and Examination Council, having given us the GCSE, is now preparing to administer the coup-de-grace to A-levels. In the consultation document on A-levels of September 1990 which Mr MacGregor had called for earlier, the Schools Examination and Assessment Council speaks of a 'broad and balanced curriculum' for post-16 students giving all a clearer and better system of opportunity. But beware the phrases 'broad and balanced', 'for all' and 'better opportunity'. Such language usually presages an assault on education. 'Breadth and balance' means the loss of depth; 'for all students' means that courses have to survive the scrutiny of professional anti-racists and anti-sexists; while 'better opportunities' means that anything which cannot be done by all will be done by none.

And so it proves in this case. In a reversal of roles, what were called AS (i.e. 'Advanced Supplementary') examinations are now to dictate the nature and content of advanced examinations. AS syllabuses (one half the length of A-level syllabuses, and represented one sixth of a sixth former's time) are to embody 'the essential skills, knowledge and learning which constitute the advanced level standard'.

Without accusing the Schools Examination and Assessment

Council of deliberate disingenuousness, it is impossible to see how half a course can cover even the essentials of a whole course without dilution of the subject. Worries on this score are compounded further by reading in the document that what are now called simple A courses will merely provide 'additional contexts' in which students can illustrate their grasp of a discipline. In subjects such as physics, mathematics, history, classics and philosophy, it is hardly possible to distinguish between essential content and additional contexts, between core and periphery. The inevitable result of these proposals is that students will come to degree courses less well prepared and less knowledgeable than at present.

All the current anti-academic nostrums are in fact enshrined in the proposals: insistence on cross-curricula themes, relevance to working life, core skills, and mandatory course work assessment, together with the ritual obeisances to the alleged linguistic and cultural diversity of our nation and the demand to avoid 'gender, ethnic, age and other forms of bias'. None of this can enhance the academic content of the course, and none of it is relevant to a genuine academic discipline.

Teacher Training

Where does all this anti-academic prejudice in education stem from and how is it that it has gained such a foothold in the higher reaches of education? In conversation, many people have suggested to me that the root cause of our trouble is the way we prepare teachers for their profession. I have heard of public school headmasters who prefer not to take graduates of colleges and departments of education because of the egalitarian, anti-elitist and child-centered attitudes to education which are promulgated in such places. He adds that schools in the maintained sector have not had the luxury of such a choice. And despite the introduction of the licensed teacher scheme, whereby a few mature graduates in some subjects are allowed to train as teachers in schools without having to undergo formal teacher training, it is still the case that the vast majority of teachers have to spend time taking either a B.Ed. degree or a Postgraduate Certificate of Education in a college or department of education. There is much that is objectionable in this requirement.

For example, in many Education courses it is taught that equality of outcome is a proper educational goal and that subject curricula are open to criticism to the extent that they do not promote this goal. In many colleges of education it is almost impossible for students or others to challenge the consensus on comprehensivization and mixed-ability teaching. (In one case which came to my attention, a mild remark from a student on the problems involved in such teaching was crushed by the response 'So you're in favour of educational apartheid'.)

Further, it is clear that teaching is a practical ability, best learned by doing; educational theory — even of a more elevated sort than the type just referred to — has no direct bearing on this ability. The government has attempted to enhance the academic or subject content of B.Ed. degrees, by insisting that more time is spent on teaching would-be teachers the actual subjects they will be teaching, as opposed to educational theory and pedagogy. But, as is suggested by Sheila Lawlor in *Teachers Mistaught* (CPS 1990), these efforts have to some considerable degree been undermined by the ruse of redirecting what ought to be the academic part of the B.Ed. towards the interests and methods of current educational theory and practice. The situation, indeed, is so bad that *The Guardian* reported on December 4th 1990 of a group of final year would-be language teachers at Roehampton Institute dismally failing to display 'the working knowledge of language structure' (i.e. grammar) which, according to *The Guardian*, they will shortly be expected by Her Majesty's Inspectors to teach in school.

The only real way to reform teacher education would be to open the teaching profession to graduates who have a good knowledge of their subjects and who prefer to learn how to teach in schools willing to induct them, rather than spending time in a college or department of education. Such indeed has been my view for some time, but until recently I had been reluctant to see teacher education as positively harmful, rather than simply time-wasting.

The recent case of Mrs Annis Garfield, however, suggests a disturbing possibility: that teacher training may in fact be acting not just as a possibly inefficient means of indoctrinating would-be teachers with anti-elitist, anti-educational prejudices; but that it may actually be a means of filtering out would-be teachers who manifest academic talent (and, doubtless and conversely, a way of filtering in applicants with 'one of the languages of London's speech communities', as one college prospectus inimitably has it).

Coming from a strongly academic background, Mrs Garfield is a graduate in classics from Cambridge, a former O- and A-level examiner who wants to train as a teacher. She believes in teaching reading through phonics, in the teaching of grammar and in making children do worthwhile things in school even if they don't want to. But she has been rejected by five departments of education, none of which, so far as I know, has any particular reputation for extremism of any sort in the educational world. Has she been rejected despite, or because of, what she is and what she believes? My suspicion is the latter, a suspicion reinforced by hearing of other, similar cases since hers received national publicity in September 1990, and also by the offers of interview Mrs Garfield received for a bogus application sent under the name of Ms Sharon Shrill, a black Sociology graduate who spells 'education' 'eductation' and 'acquire' 'aquire'. In contrast to Ms Shrill, everything Mrs Garfield stands for is counter to the dogmas which hold sway in departments of education and, through them, in much of the teaching profession generally.

At Nene College, Mrs Garfield was told she would have been better off with a qualification in craft than a degree in classics and that she ought to seek a job as a dinner lady, while Ms Shrill's 'qualification' was found more relevant to primary teaching. At Nene, students in the B.Ed. course undertake 'a first exploration of egalitarian issues, in respect, for example, of differences of gender, race and social background'. Neither the appalling prose nor the doctrinaire insistence on egalitarianism as a key educational issue are peculiar to Nene College; both are indicative of what will be found in many, if not most, education departments. It is this doctrinaire egalitarianism that has been in large measure responsible for the mediocrity enforced in so many of our schools, where group work and social levelling are preferred to individual excellence.

Mrs Garfield's views on the teaching of reading apparently did not find favour at Oxford Polytechnic, while her declared preference for Jane Austen and Shakespeare over Caribbean litera- ture produced an 'unreceptive' reaction at Warwick University. Again, these responses are entirely symptomatic of the ideology of child-centredness, thanks to which many primary schools are largely indistinguishable from play groups, and in some undisciplined secondary schools, pupils and staff jointly determine school policy on matters of discipline.

Personal and Social Education

Let us be frank: academic and didactic attitudes are being swept out of state education. Nowhere is this more apparent than in the growth of what is called Personal and Social Education. PSE (to use the acronym adopted by the establishment) is distinguished not so much by its content (for it has none) as by its manner and its motivation. Its manner is that of the do-it-yourself self-esteem kit of popular American psychology. Its goal is to direct attention away from subjects to the child itself. In this it is symptomatic of all the anti- educational tendencies which currently afflict us.

Each one of us is formed through entry into already existing cultural traditions. Thought and expression can begin only when the individual has mastered the means to thinks or express himself. If we are genuinely concerned to give the child the ability to articulate his inner self with any real depth or sensitivity, we cannot underes- timate the importance of rote learning and of the study of the classics of our literature. A child is not likely to invent from his own resources what it has taken generations to formulate and discover. Formal schooling is justified to the extent that it transmits to children the fruits gathered by preceding generations. It is worse than a waste of time if it is regarded — as in PSE as a time for self-exploration or self-discovery. Until the self is situated within a cultural tradition, there is nothing to explore, no direction to any discovery, and nothing to express or articulate.

We, as educators, merely patronise the child by making his unformed personality the subject of our attention. Yet such is the aim in PSE. Children, being uneducated, are in no position to make judgments on their goals or motivations or on what they are being taught or on their teachers. Yet PSE makes the child's personality and its reactions the focus of attention, and often in a way which would rightly have been regarded as unprofessional in the past. This is not just a distraction from other subjects, although it certainly is that when, as happens, scholarship pupils even in academic schools have to forgo coaching in their chosen subject to attend PSE sessions. But, worse than merely wasting time, PSE turns the child's gaze inwards when it should be looking outwards. PSE question-naires invite children to comment on how their friends see them and how they see their friends, a form of analysis likely to exacerbate worries and anxieties in nervous pupils. Others invite children to say what their reaction would be were they to discover that their mother is having an affair with a neighbour, a form of enquiry many parents would rightly find offensive. Above all, PSE has the potential to poison that disinterested and mind-expanding attention to the best which characterises a truly educational engagement. It prefers sessions of cosy and manipulative introspection in which both pupil and teacher are required to play demeaning and conspiratorial roles. Yet many schools now make willingness to undertake PSE work a requirement in the appointment of new teachers.

Censorship

There are, naturally, many teachers who object to the policies currently being promulgated throughout the maintained sector of education. I know that there are, because many have written to me in response to articles of mine to say this, and I have no doubt, too, that many others agree with them. But many of those who write to me are either leaving the profession or keeping their heads down and their opinions to themselves. They know that speaking out publicly against a fashionable trend in education is professional death. (And dissenting teachers do not write only to me. One of the few heartening features of the whole depressing situation is the way Melanie Phillips in *The Guardian* has over the last year taken up the cause of free speech in education, following responses to articles of hers from teachers too afraid to speak publicly.)

In some ways, this is the most intractable feature of the whole situation. It is surely indefensible in a civilized society that those who point out problems and raise questions are censored and censured by their colleagues and supervisors. In education there is a crisis. This is widely admitted. Yet those who are thoughtful and who care enough about education openly to suggest causes for the crisis are threatened with the prospect of losing their jobs should their diagnosis offend current orthodoxy.

There are, of course, the well-publicized cases of censorship, such as that of Ray Honeyford, who lost his job because he publicly questioned the multi-cultural policy of his local authority. There is also the case of Chris McGovern and Anthony Freeman, history teachers in Lewes, who under a Conservative local authority, have effectively lost their posts for daring to raise doubts about GCSE history (doubts, incidentally, which people in government share). With Robert Skidelsky, McGovern and Freeman have gone on to set up the History Curriculum Association to promote their view of history teaching, and have received declarations of support from many other teachers in all sections and levels of teaching, but frequently with the proviso that the support must remain anonymous. And finally, there is the case of Martin Turner, the educational psychologist who pointed to an unprecedented decline in reading standards in primary schools and was ordered not to speak publicly — again, be it noted, by superiors in a Conservative-controlled education authority. But over and above the well-publicized cases, we must see as victims of censorship every teacher in any school who is castigated by the Head for speaking out against 'management' policies, and who is dubbed 'uncommitted', 'insecure', 'frightened' or 'negative' for doing so. And we must also remember every teacher who is aware of the way many of our educational attitudes are betraying the young, but who is afraid to say so; and finally all those who have left the profession because of its lack of intellectual freedom and honesty.

In considering censorship in education, we must also take into account the way the educational establishment closes ranks, when faced by outside criticism, attempting to deflect opprobrium on to the heads of the critics. Thus, as Caroline Cox and John Marks tell us in *The Insolence of Office* (Claridge Press, 1989), when work they published challenged educational orthodoxy on the effectiveness of comprehensive schools, DES officials attempted to discredit their research, and it was only with great difficulty that they were able to vindicate their reputations. Similarly, in December 1990, when an official from the Abbey National Building Society in Milton Keynes commented adversely on television on the inability of school leavers to spell or calculate, officers in Buckinghamshire County Council claimed that the official in question had left the firm in disgruntlement; and then, when challenged, that she had been demoted. Both these claims were untrue, and denied by the Building Society, which said that their official was indeed expressing company concern over educational standards in trainees. But incidents such as these show the degree to which educational officialdom is prepared to smear its critics.

The Inspectorate is allowed to criticize what happens in classrooms, and the classroom teacher is made to shoulder the blame. Yet, often enough, the classroom teacher is only doing what he or she has been 'advised' to do by the Inspectors and ordered to do by the various Curriculum and Examination Councils and the DES. But if the classroom teacher is incautious enough to point this out publicly, or even in a staff meeting, he can expect the full weight of the educational establishment to fall on his head. He can certainly forget about promotion or advancement within the state system of education. One senior teacher wrote to me *à propos* a piece of mine on core skills, complaining that the day was fast approaching when teachers would be spending their time observing their pupils, rather than teaching them. But, she added, 'there would be no interest in my writing to *The Daily Telegraph* (on this) unless I were able to state my position and place of employment and that, no doubt, would be a quick way to *un*employment'. So most do not speak out, and simply bottle up their anger at the system. But, as Melanie Phillips correctly observes, 'how can children be educated in any meaningful sense of the word, if their teachers are intellectually fettered and cowed?'

Democracy and Education

I am not very interested in the opinions of Her Majesty's Inspectors and educational researchers on current educational standards. Their reports are couched largely in terms of the current orthodoxies and accept current targets as the ones to which we should flight our arrows. Before 1914, historians tell us, although the school leaving age was 14, there was near universal literacy and numeracy in this country; school-leavers from all social classes had a good knowledge of the Bible, an acquaintance with national classics of literature and with their own history. It is not so much that we fail to reach our targets these days (though we do). What is more interesting is to understand why we fail to do what was done before 1914. Might it not be because education itself is now misconceived?

British Society before 1914 was in many ways democratic. There was universal male suffrage, and there were mass circulation newspapers and periodicals of a far higher standard than their successors of today. But society had not yet taken on the manners of egalitarian democracy, the lack of deference to one's betters so characteristic of collectivism, or the denial of authority in every area of life.

It may be that the era immediately before 1914 was the last

time a genuine education for the whole population was possible. Although, in the name of democracy, there was an attempt to educate everyone, everyone was also sufficiently deferential, sufficiently reverential towards what was higher, as to make true education possible. The delicate and potentially destructive relationship between democratic manners and education is not, of course, something which was unknown in earlier times. Plato's *Republic* is the profoundest treatise ever written on education; not the least of its virtues is the stunningly accurate picture it gives of manners and of teachers in a certain type of democracy:

> The father accustoms himself to become like his child and to fear his sons, and the son in his desire for freedom becomes like his father and has no fear or reverence for his parent. Metic is like citizen, and citizen like metic, and stranger like both ... and there are other trifles of this kind. The schoolmaster fears and flatters his pupils, and the pupils despise both their schoolmasters and their tutors. And altogether, the young act like their seniors, and compete with them in speech and action; while the old men condescend to the young and become triumphs of versatility and wit, imitating their juniors in order to avoid the appearance of being sour or despotic. (562-563)

There cannot be true education without a pinch of sourness, a hint of despotism and a willingness to revere; for all these things are necessary to bend the lawless and turbulent spirit of the young to the forces which ought to master them.

The current orthodoxy is that young people should 'appraise critically the received notions and methodologies of their disciplines.' These words are taken from the document put out by the Schools' Examination and Assessment Council, proposing to halve the academic content of sixth form syllabuses. The assumption is that seventeen or eighteen year olds, after 130 hours of study, will be in a position to do what even Einstein, Nietzsche or Schoenberg could not do until well into their twenties. But then the current orthodoxy in education is infused with egalitarian ideals and rhetoric. It cannot bear the thought that there is something which a teenager could not 'critically appraise' after a cursory introduction.

Rather than teaching pupils to criticize their disciplines, educators should begin — and perhaps end — by leading them to respect and love what they are learning about. They should build on the natural sense of curiosity and interest young people have in many things, and teach them to regard our forms of knowledge as what they are: achievements won by the patient work of great men and women and which will not be won by the young without the exercise of a comparable patience and discipline. Criticism has its place in any discipline, but in the absence of true knowledge, it is jejune and shallow, and likely to quench the desire to learn. What, indeed, is the point of studying a discipline if what we are aiming at from the start is the ability to criticise its received notions and methodology? Wouldn't we be better off studying something whose received notions and methodology were worth cherishing as genuinely revelatory of the world and of human experience, something which the pupil can find pleasure in learning, and the teacher in teaching, and to which the pupil is ready to attend?

This, though, is not the view of Her Majesty's Inspectors of schools, who will tear into any school whose pupils are not in continual conversation with their teachers, and where the pupils are not continually questioning everything they are taught. In 1989 they lectured King Edward VI School at Stratford-on-Avon, a school they admitted had excellent records in academic achievement and behaviour, for its reliance on 'traditional' methods. According to the Inspectors 'the needs of the pupils in the late 20th century requires the introduction of new procedures, new methods and new courses'. The Inspectors note that in lessons at Stratford pupils listen 'attentively' and, even worse, sometimes with 'evident enjoyment'. This clearly cannot be allowed to go on. The Inspectorate is hostile to the habit of attending to matters recognised by pupils and teachers alike to be more important than the personalities of either. They would destroy a situation in which reverence for a subject could develop, in order to promote instead the self-expression and chatter of the young. Their aim is not to create educated minds, but to introduce into uneducated minds the illusion that they contain opinions that others might be interested in hearing.

The Inspectors are applying, in fact, the educational philosophy of John Dewey, the American philosopher and educationist who has been so influential throughout the English-speaking world. Dewey was in turn following the teaching of Rousseau. For both, what was crucial in education was the child's interest. Education, they held, could succeed only to the extent that it was relevant to what the child already knew. For Dewey, real learning could arise only in the attempt to answer some problem the child already recognised and was worried by. Instead of seeing education as opening up new and broader worlds for the child, worlds for whose rules, methods and content the child had to prepare himself by means of instruction from without, Dewey believed that teaching which was not immediately relevant to some problem the child perceived as a problem was bound to be ineffective. It would simply result in the transmission of 'inert' knowledge, useless to child and teacher alike. Hence the stress in Dewey's educational writings, and in the schools with which he was associated, on project-work, activity and problem solving.

Dewey's philosophy is the basis of current theories of teaching, and is enshrined in institutions of teacher-training in this country. It is the reason why in those places, and in education generally, content is so often sacrificed to method and technique. It is the basis of the belief that there are 'study skills' which can be acquired in the absence of content and knowledge. It is the basis of all the educational practice which stresses play, discovery, activity and 'student-centered' learning and, which, like the Inspectorate, decries 'passive' learning and 'didactic' teaching.

In Dewey we also find sentimental talk of the value of the experience of the child, of 'the intrinsic significance of every growing experience'. In what Dewey would regard as the spirit of true democracy, classrooms are to become miniature Swiss cantons, in which everything is up for discussion and negotiation by the whole population. The teacher is no more than a provider of 'suggestions', a 'facilitator' in today's jargon. The facilitator's suggestions are not a 'mould for a cast-iron result', according to Dewey's *Experience and Education* of 1938; they are 'a starting point to be developed into a plan through contributions from the experience of all engaged in the learning process'.

Dewey's democracy, being based on an egalitarian conception of the worth of different types of experience, was bound to enshrine mediocrity. To his credit, he at least made no bones about this consequence, any more than Rousseau had done earlier in recognising that his political proposals would promote a mediocrity of achievement. In his *Democracy and Education* of 1916 Dewey criticized the development of the inner personality on the grounds that what cannot be fully and freely communicated was *eo ipso* futile and rotten. In class-divided societies, and societies with social and intellectual élites, the culture of the upper classes is necessarily sterile and artificial, according to Dewey. The ideal form of social existence is one in which everything is shared by all, including intellectual and cultural life. So in schools the curriculum must be selected with an emphasis on those things which can interest the widest possible group. And as the group includes children, their interests and problems have as much right to be heard and focused on as those of 'educated' adults. Hence, in Dewey, child or student-centered learning goes hand in hand with group work, as part of an overall political and social project.

I have no doubt that the popularity of Dewey's ideas among current teacher trainers and the educational establishment is also in a broad sense political, and is based on a particular conception of democracy. According to the practice of the School of Education at Roehampton Institute (which is one of the largest teacher-training institutes in the country) children should have the right to 'negotiate' their curriculum and timetable. The assistant dean of education defends the practice in this way: 'Negotiated curriculum is an idea rooted in a concept of democracy. There is a lot of evidence to suggest that children as young as three are better motivated if they have a say in the way their day is organised.'

After twenty years or more of this sort of thing it is not

surprising that we are currently witnessing the biggest fall in reading standards for over 40 years; that one million young people between the ages of 16 and 20 admit they cannot read properly; that three and a half million adults have problems with simple addition, subtraction, multiplication and division. Nor is it surprising that spending in real terms on education has gone up by 42% per child since 1979. The general lowering of standards at the top end of education has not resulted in any improvement in standards at the bottom end, but quite the reverse; it has also raised the cost of schooling since the worse things get, the more those responsible lay claim to the resources which (in their view) are the only remedy.

It is highly plausible to see the egalitarianism which stems from the teachings of Dewey as the proximate cause of our educational decline (and seeing this might lead his followers to question the underlying concept of democracy). The insistence on giving everyone the same education, embraced first in comprehensivization, and then in the GCSE (promoted as one examination for all) and which will be yet further set in stone in the statutory National Curriculum, has resulted in a universal mediocrity. The best are given a watered-down academic curriculum, as a result of which universities are having to consider extending their courses and lowering their standards. But this watered-down academic curriculum has done little to address the needs of the bottom 40% either. It has produced widespread dissatisfaction among them (as is shown by truancy rates in secondary schools) and it has not led to their learning the basic elements of their language, of their history or of mathematics.

But there is, underlying our educational malaise, something deeper than Dewey's sentimental egalitarianism. This deeper cause is an attitude which would be regarded as admirable by many who do not share Dewey's egalitarianism; it is therefore worth according separate treatment to it. It is what might be called Socratism: the idea that education ought primarily to be about inducing a spirit of criticism in the young. In the following section I will develop an argument to show that such an aim can only undermine true education; true education must be conceived in quite a different way. (In the Appendix I relate what I say here to Socrates and his classical critics and successors.)

True Education

Education is no doubt about the development of reason; but this is quite a different thing from instilling a critical spirit. For without possessing reason in a sense deeper than that implied by most talk of 'the critical attitude', a young person is unable to distinguish between good criticisms and bad criticisms. As George Orwell remarked in *Inside the Whale*: 'Patriotism, religion, the Empire, the family, the sanctity of marriage, the Old School Tie, birth, breeding, honour, discipline — anyone of ordinary education could turn the whole lot of them inside out in three minutes.' But it would not follow that 'anyone' would be right to do this, nor indeed that 'ordinary education' should aim at producing any such result. That it so often does is no point in its favour.

In fact, reason presupposes a proper training in attitude and morality. Reason in the correct sense is not the readiness of any uneducated or half-educated person to hold forth on things he does not understand, nor even the readiness of an educated person to demand explicit justification for practices which stand in no obvious need of it. What I mean by 'reason' might better be characterised as right reason or reasonableness — in order to distinguish it from sophistry and that barrack-room litigiousness which would adduce 'reasons' in support of what is neither good nor worthy nor true. It is a good thing that people understand what they are doing, that they come to their own reasoned conclusions, that they act on reason rather than on blind instinct or impetuous desire. But we must also understand the way in which our reasoning powers are embedded in a way of life, and that there is no clear-cut distinction between reason and emotion. We must appreciate that reasoning on any matter quickly comes to an end, when one reaches principles which cannot be further justified. But how do we reach agreement on this point?

And how do we ensure that the right principles are agreed on?

To both questions, the answer is the same: by belonging to a community whose members are habitually disposed to choose and to be motivated by the good, the true and the beautiful. It is for this reason that education becomes a central philosophical concern: in some ways *the* central concern. If philosophy seeks for the good, the true and the beautiful, then it will at the same time be delineating the curriculum of a good education; but by a sublimely virtuous circle, this means that only those already educated in the right way, only those who have the correct moral and intellectual training will be in a position to philosophise. We must also distinguish between wisdom and mere cleverness, and understand that cleverness in itself is no defence against wickedness and, indeed, is often deployed in the cause of wickedness.

Current educational orthodoxy would have it had we should encourage children, who are as yet unformed human beings and a prey to desire and passion, to make their own decisions and judgments about education. It is hardly surprising that the result is a decline not only in educational standards, but also in behaviour. Is this substitution of a child-centered cleverness for a disciplined education an inevitable consequence of democratic customs seeping ever further down the age-range? Or is it possible to have a society run on democratic principles by adult citizens, united by respect for a form of education which recognises that there is a best in human affairs, and which recognises too that children need a thorough training in that best before they will be in a position to perceive it? Surely, we must acquire the habits of virtue, for we are certainly not born with them. And we have to *acquire* them, rather than reason about them, because before a certain age we are not in any position to reason about anything. Intelligence develops more slowly than our desires and passions and physique; and until someone is well into his maturity he will lack the experience of life with which to judge wisely on things of importance.

It is not difficult to extend what has been said about virtue to other areas of education, both intellectual and cultural. No one is born with a grasp of arithmetic or spelling or French irregular verbs. The abilities to read, write, spell, calculate, speak foreign languages and so on have to be acquired before one can do anything worthwhile with them. (This point one would have thought too elementary to have to make were it not for the current craze for 'real books' in primary school: a kind of licensed insanity in which it is assumed that children will acquire a taste for reading by being surrounded by books and reading materials without being actually taught to read.)

It is not only basic skills which the learner has to acquire before he can appreciate what he is to do with them. The taste for history, for music, for art, for physics, for biology, for literature and for most other subjects is one that is only understood and hence only acquired by those who have already gone some distance in the subjects, and who understand what it is they have to offer and the precise nature of their attractions. These points are obvious enough for physical pursuits, such as skiing or snorkelling or riding, where they are widely recognised to hold; but they are no less true of intellectual pursuits, in which understanding goes along with depth of knowledge. And a positive attitude to a subject will be better induced in pupils by a teacher who himself has a reverence and enthusiasm for his subject, than by one who is constantly carping at the *status quo* or by one who is so lacking in authority or confidence that he is forever seeking the opinions of his pupils on matters in which he should be far better qualified than they.

Induction into an intellectual discipline requires the learner to submit to the habits of that discipline, uncritically if need be. Only in this way will he acquire the knowledge to reason effectively about the subject, and the wisdom to reason correctly. For it is only when a person has the elements of the sciences and the humane disciplines in his grasp that he can be said to be fully rational and able to discourse properly on those matters which concern us as human beings. But in order to get into this happy state, he must first submit to the disciplines of study, so learning how to speak and reason. The rational human being is formed by instruction from without, by acquiring the wherewithal to enter what Oakeshott called the conversations of mankind. And, as we learn from Aristotle (*Politics*, 1253a 7-17), it is the ability to speak rationally to one's fellows — speech as opposed to voice — which distinguishes man from the animals, which makes political activity possible and which forms the basis on which we will educate the as yet not fully rational members of our species.

Some people see all this as a paradox. How is it, they say, that rationality depends on the uncritical acquisition of certain habits of thought and feeling? But this is a paradox only to those who hold a false view of thinking and reasoning, and who do not realise that both are part of already existing conversations. Children must attain gradual mastery of some of the areas in which people have thought and through which they have expressed themselves. A child's rationality develops through joining in conversations which both preceded his birth and will (if education succeeds) survive his death.

If I do not see paradox in my account of learning and of rationality, nor do I see objectionable authoritarianism. It is authoritarian, and necessarily so, in the recognition that the newcomer in any area is not an isolated ego, able to assess everything for himself before joining the world of human discourse. The opposite view can be found in much seventeenth- and eighteenth-century philosophy. It is neither philosophically nor psychologically plausible, but its legacy remains with us in the notion of child-centred education. Many advocates of child-centred education would claim to be anti-individualist and opposed to the idea that the human person is at root an isolated ego. But they are thoroughly individualistic in thinking that the child uninitiated into the several scientific and humane disciplines might be able to think and choose for himself.

Against the philosophical individualism which, despite appearances, so dominates current educational thinking and which places an unfair and unbearable burden on the child, we must insist on a genial and unoppressive authoritarianism. It is genial because the child who masters the disciplines of education is to that extent liberated. It is unoppressive because the conversations of mankind are neither static nor fixed, but continue and develop as newcomers contribute to them. But even a genial and unoppressive authoritarianism requires confidence on the part of those in authority in the value and nature of their task. Nothing is more symptomatic of our current educational failure than the protestations of so many of our educators that they and their methods are unauthoritarian, and that they are devolving responsibility to their pupils. This new orthodoxy is neither genial nor unoppressive; it suggests nothing less than a loss of faith on the part of those who should have faith, and whose lack of faith deprives their pupils of a genuine intellectual liberation. But make no mistake about it: as we have seen, the new orthodoxy is in another way thoroughly authoritarian. Workers in Scholesia who do not conspire in this collective lack of faith are liable to be unceremoniously dumped over the border.

There are several ways which the authoritarian aspect of true education makes it inegalitarian. It is inegalitarian as between teachers and pupils. It is inegalitarian in that the disciplines are seen as deriving their authority from the best work done in them, and from the judgments of those who are internally recognised as best. It is inegalitarian in that there is no presumption that the best, most authoritative work in a discipline should be accessible to everyone, even to everyone in the educated public. True education, then, rests on the existence of a public prepared to accept the judgments of authorities in various fields, without itself being able effectively to criticize these authorities, or their 'received notions and methodologies'. And notwithstanding my gloom about the decline of deference in our society, there is clear evidence that the general public still prefers the style of education in which teachers are seen as genuinely authoritative, and in which students and pupils actually learn things, rather than acquiring a universal scepticism.

Egalitarian Centralism

This could be, of course, because the public as a whole is still sufficiently inegalitarian in spirit to be willing, on occasion, to defer to recognised authorities, and to accept as a fact of life that there are unbridgeable differences of aspiration and attainment between human beings, differences which ought to be reflected in the education a child is offered. Such an authoritarian conception of education is not shared by those who administer education, for whom the words 'élite' and 'élitism' have become, by one of those moral inversions with which students of collectivist organisations are so familiar, terms of abuse. This may seem a strong thing to say; but what, other than blind egalitarianism, could explain the establishment's unshakeable opposition to letting the excellent excel in primary schools, and its unshakeable commitment to comprehensivization, the GCSE, the replacement of 'A' levels by yet another 'examination for all' and an extensive and centrally directed National Curriculum?

Whether a bureaucracy motivated in this way is an inevitable consequence of modern democracy is a moot point. Something similar, indeed, has happened to the Arts Council in its decline since the days of Keynes and Clark — men who had a clear vision of what they thought of as the best in the arts, and of their duty (not merely their right) to impose this vision through the State. Nowadays, the Arts Council is filled with bureaucrats, who lack vision themselves and who are unprepared to make judgments of quality. Instead, they endeavour to select for subsidy and promotion works which they take to mirror the social and ethnic constitution of society as a whole. For them too, as for our educators, the idea that their proper role might be a paternalist one is little more than a bad joke.

Whether egalitarian centralism is an inevitable feature of mass democracies or only of the bureaucracies which tend to grow in them is hard to say. What seems quite clear, however, is that the only way in which a better vision of education can flourish is by removing it as far as possible from the hands of a bureaucracy which conceives its role in egalitarian terms. By speaking of the bureaucracy in this context, I wish specifically to include not only the examining authorities, the Inspectors and those in charge of framing the National Curriculum — all of whom seem hell-bent on forcing every child into a uniform and uniformly mediocre educational mould — but also those currently in charge of teacher training, where in college after college and department after department the egalitarian message is put across, and equality of opportunity is judged in terms of equality of outcome. In these institutions, as we have seen, whether success-rates in a given course mirror the social mix of society as a whole is *always* taken to be a relevant consideration in judging a curriculum. Education is no longer seen as an end in itself, but rather as an instrument of social engineering. True education, however, should be a time of blessed release from social and political 'realities', during which teachers and learners find pleasure and enrichment in what they do.

The vision of education I would advocate is one which is frankly authoritarian. By virtue of its authoritarian standpoint it is far more inclined to stress the need to inculcate the right dispositions, tastes and virtues in our children, and far less inclined to base education on the tastes, judgments and supposed critical faculties of the pupils themselves. It is also a vision which recognises that not everyone can progress as far as everyone else in any particular subject, and which sees progress in a subject as dependent on the demands of the subject, rather than on irrelevant social or political issues.

Divisiveness

We have to accept that there are ineradicable differences between human beings regarding intellect and motivation. Attempting to play down these differences in education as we have done over the past 30 years has helped the bottom 40% no more than it has helped the academically gifted. In Germany, at secondary level, the *Hauptschüle* do not attempt to provide a watered-down academic curriculum for those who are not academically motivated. They provide a genuinely work-directed training instead, and value it appropriately. Rather than following this example, our educationists wish to alter institutions and courses designed for an academic clientele so as to allow wider 'access' to them. But why should there be wider access to successful academic institutions and courses if that entails changing them, rather than access to different institutions and differently oriented courses? Such a suggestion may be 'élitist', 'divisive', 'inegalitarian' and 'undemocratic': but that only shows that those words ought not to be understood as terms of abuse, but rather as descriptive of the true educational endeavour.

We need, then, an education system which is divisive, élitist and inegalitarian. Whether it is undemocratic in an objectionable sense depends on whether it is objectionable from a democratic point of view for teachers to accept responsibility for the standards they are charged with upholding; or whether it is less democratic to respect differences between different types of individual, than to force everyone into the same mediocre mould. No doubt people will give different answers to these questions, depending on their different conceptions of democracy. I have to say that a conception of democracy which does not allow for real distinctions between people, or for real authority in education and culture, is not worth having, though one which does is very much worth having. The key question is how divisiveness, élitism and inequality can be brought back into our educational system. Giving more power to the bureaucracy in the shape of statutory control of the curriculum and examinations is clearly not the answer. Bureaucracies are inevitably happier with judgments of quantity rather than of quality, and this is as true in the field of education as in any other.

The Remedy?

The free-market approach to education is to enable parents to choose schools effectively. On this view schools shall be taken out of local authority control and funded according to the pupils they attract (either by means of vouchers given to parents or by direct funding from central government relative to their pupil numbers). I am not convinced that a free-market will by itself solve all our problems. After all, we have a free market in music, with results which are far from universally good. In fact there is a strange irony here. For if the free-market provides and promotes the music which corrupts taste, it is those educators who are avowedly egalitarian and who would base education on what they see as relevant to the child's existing interests and tastes who put pop music on the curriculum. As all serious theorists of the market — from Adam Smith to Hayek — realise, we must look outside the market for institutions to uphold morality and taste. The market by itself is simply the most efficient and responsive means we have discovered to enable people to realise their preferences. But it says nothing about those preferences or how to evaluate them.

The State itself and its leaders have lost the will to act with authority in matters of education and taste, perhaps because they are afraid of offending voters, or perhaps because they lack the necessary knowledge. Our public-sector institutions of education have fallen into the hands of bureaucrats and theorists imbued with a collectivist spirit. My doubts notwithstanding, a free-market approach at least offers the possibility of more diversity than currently exists. It offers the possibility of types of education more suited to particular needs, and of the flourishing of genuine educational excellence in different areas.

When it comes to the education of their own children, most parents, however collectivist and non-élitist their principles may be in general, want their children educated appropriately. They would like their children to learn what it is good for them to know. Given the chance, most parents would, I believe, choose in a wiser and more responsible way than an irresponsive bureaucracy, with one eye always on the mass and never on the individual, and, as we learn from public choice theory, with its other eye on its own good and self-presentation, and never on that of the recipient of its services. As the figures quoted earlier show, the educational bureaucracy has been extremely good at serving its own interests, but less good at serving those of others. It is worth remembering that some of the most vehement criticism of the unlamented Inner London Education Authority came from West Indian parents who could see in concrete detail just how much their children were being let down by their schools, despite (or rather because of) the commitment in those schools to child-centeredness, 'relevance' and anti-racism. And I know plenty of 'committed' socialists who have their children educated outside the state system, just as I know of few government ministers who send their children to state schools.

As things stand at the moment, only a free-market approach to education, together with a repeal of those parts of the Education Reform Act which have put the curriculum and examinations in the hands of collectivist bureaucrats, offers any chance that true educational values will re-emerge in those schools available to the majority of the population. That my optimism here and my belief in the pertinence of the authoritarian view of education are not wholly misguided, is demonstrated by the fact that it is precisely where parents are free to chose the education of their children that such a vision of education flourishes.

Some may find my advocacy of authoritative and authoritarian forms of education in tension with my advocacy of more diversity and choice and less state control. On closer inspection, I believe, there is no real contradiction. It is a general maxim that what a government directly controls it cannot resist interfering with, and this is as true of conservative as it is of socialist governments. In interfering with an institution, governments all too often have ends in view which are in conflict with the long-term well-being of the institution and in conflict with its proper ends. An instructive analogy here might be the German Federal Bank which, in contrast to the Bank of England, is constitutionally independent of the government and has as a result been able to provide more long-term support to German industry and commerce than has ever been enjoyed by British businessmen. Be that as it may, governments, conservative and socialist, persistently interfere with education for purposes of social engineering or of manpower planning; while one set of politicians sees education as a means of reducing social divisions, the other set is obsessed with its relevance to the needs of the economy. Under either type of pressure the true ends of education are likely to be lost sight of. Indeed, those nowadays promoting education for enterprise propose just the same nostrums as did the radicals of the '60s: child-centered learning, project work and group problem-solving. This is hardly surprising, given that many of yesterday's radicals are today's 'educators for enterprise', who have no more understanding of education now than they did in their previous incarnations.

The goals of true education are to give a training in morality and taste, to inculcate certain basic abilities and attitudes, and to provide for a disinterested study of the best that has been thought and said, for those who are able or willing to profit from it. Educational imperatives and authority do not derive from the plans of politicians or the dreams of bureaucrats. They derive from the basic human needs of children and from the disciplines and forms of knowledge to be imparted to them. It should be obvious to anyone who has observed the educational scene for the past twenty years that the best hope of keeping educational imperatives safe is by keeping our institutions of education at one remove from the hands of government. The most straightforward way of doing this is to allow schools to develop free of governmental interference and to allow parents to decide between successful and unsuccessful schools.

Allowing parents genuine choice of school is not, then, inconsistent with authoritarian styles of education. The freedom from government interference entailed by revoking the National Curriculum and the statutory examination system and by allowing schools to develop in their own way, subject to parental choice rather than local or central government control, is, as things stand, the best way to allow such styles of education to flourish. It would also permit greater diversity and selectivity on the part of the schools, something which a governmentally directed system of education would at present find very hard to introduce, but which is essential to any genuine reform of our educational system. Public opinion surveys show most parents to be in favour of grammar schools (still), but most parents would object to a formal re-introduction of the 11+ (despite evidence to show that children in secondary modern schools often do better than their peers in comprehensive schools). A re-introduction of the 11+ and the re-erection of a rigid distinction between grammar and secondary modern schools may well be politically and socially unacceptable. But a better way than either the grammar-secondary modern school system or the present universal comprehensivization suggests itself. Under a system of independent schools funded in terms of pupil demand, schools would start to develop to cater for particular types of pupils, some more academic, some more artistic, some more work-oriented, and so on, and they would recruit accordingly. In this way, what is now politically impossible (when all schools are directed by the state bureaucracy which conceives its democratic duty to be to make all schools cater for all pupils), becomes practically and painlessly possible. And, of course, within each school there is no reason why the education offered should not be seen in authoritative and authoritarian terms.

Consequences of the Proposals

a)   Examinations

With the creation of a system of effective parental choice in education, there would be little need for the vast bureaucracies and quangoes which a large state system brings into being. If those parts of the Education Reform Act which propose a national curriculum and statutory control of examinations were repealed, we could do away with the National Curriculum Council and the Schools Examination and Assessment Council at a stroke. There would still, naturally, be a need for examining boards, but these would be financed through the payment of fees for setting and marking examinations, and for awarding certificates. Schools would opt for those examining boards and examinations which had good reputations and which corresponded best to the needs of their pupils. A privatised examination system would tend to promote more diversity in types of examination, with particular needs for particular types of certificate — academic, technical, artistic — being catered for. It would also tend to push standards up, once it became clear that employers and institutions of higher education preferred the better types of qualification to inferior ones, and had the power to specify in an effective way which they preferred. Under such a régime, there would be real hope for the preservation of 'A' levels and for the restoration of 'O' levels, as well as for demanding and worthwhile trade and apprenticeship certificates. The GCSE might continue in some form, if parents, pupils and employers wanted it, but, deprived of its monopoly position, one would doubt that its softer options and lower grades would be much sought after.

b)   **The DES**

Would there be any role at all for a body like the DES in a system where, with an exception to be noted, schools were independent of direct state or local government control, financed according to their pupil numbers? Quite clearly there would be no role for a body like the DES as currently constituted, and probably no role at all for Local Education Authorities. But I would follow John Stuart Mill in asserting that even in a fully privatised system of education the state would still have two small but important duties.

Its first duty would be to protect children against feckless parents who neglected their basic education. Its second and connected duty would be to ensure that no child entered the labour market without a basic minimum knowledge of English, Mathematics and Science. I see no agency other than the state capable of fulfilling either of these duties. Only the state can force people to do anything, and only the state could enforce minimum standards in anything. If only because he was more aware than most of the dangers of the state running an education system ('a mere contrivance for moulding people to be exactly like one another'), Mill's proposals for state-enforced educational minima deserve to be taken seriously:

The instrument for enforcing the law could be no other than public examinations, extending to all children and beginning at an early age. An age might be fixed at which every child must be examined, to ascertain if he (or she) is able to read. If a child proves unable, the father, unless he has some sufficient ground of excuse, might be subjected to a modest fine ... Once in every year the examination should be renewed, with a gradually extending range of subjects, so as to make the universal acquisition, and what is more, retention, of a certain minimum of general knowledge virtually compulsory.

(J S Mill, *On Liberty*, Ch V)

Mill is proposing something like the universal testing at ages of 7, 11 and 14 of the Education Reform Act, though with more regularity and more teeth. I would dissent from Mill, though, in his suggestion that the state should itself conduct the basic tests. If the state compels children to go to school for a number of years, it must allow the people to stand in judgment over the state in the precise choice of tests and examinations. But in laying down the *minimum* standards in basic skills which private examinations are supposed to meet, and in enforcing those standards, the state would protect children and the rest of us from feckless parents and from a wholly unskilled and unemployable cadre of young people. At the same time it is important that the state's role here is, and is perceived to be, the setting of minimum targets. We have already seen enough of the National Curriculum and its workings to see the danger inherent when schools understand what should be minimum targets as maximal, and lower their sights accordingly.

In the system which I would regard as ideal, schools would be publicly financed, but self-governing. They would not be directly controlled by government, central or local. At the same time, the state is requiring that all children be educated. What would happen if in some areas, no one was prepared to run a school, or if in areas where there are plenty of schools, there were children no schools were willing to take? This is a third area where government intervention would be required, although the two types of case are rather different.

In areas where no-one else was prepared to do it, the government would itself have to set up or continue to run schools. There is, however, no reason why such schools should not eventually become self-governing, perhaps being allowed to charge higher fees from the public purse if they would be unviable under the normal economic arrangements, just as schools for the handicapped in effect already do (and would on the system I advocate continue to do). The problem of the pupil who is neither mentally nor physically handicapped, but who is still universally unacceptable, is more intractable; but I think we should wait to see how big a problem it really is before allowing it to be used as an excuse to re-invent a nationalised system of education. The least bad solution might turn out to be simply to make the taking of an appropriate proportion of such pupils one condition of a school receiving public funds. Avoidance of the danger of being labelled universally unacceptable would itself be a considerable incentive to parents and to the child itself, and might help greatly to reduce pupil indiscipline in schools.

c)   The School Leaving Age

The current cry is for more education and more access to higher education; I would suggest, however, that we seriously consider lowering the school leaving age. And I would connect this proposal to what I have said about mandatory testing of basic knowledge and abilities.

Although education is a good thing, it does not follow that everyone can profit from it at all times and at all levels, irrespective of ability and motivation. Education can, indeed, become an intolerable burden, particularly to those not suited to it when they approach adulthood. Compulsory schooling is estimated to take up about 15,000 hours of a child's time, and about half its waking life for 12 years or so. Compulsion on such a scale requires more careful justification than it commonly receives.

Anyone who has any acquaintance with secondary schools knows of the problems of pupil dissatisfaction in the fourth and fifth forms. Disruption and truancy are widespread. A few disruptive pupils can wreck a whole class for pupils and teachers alike. The radical solution to the problem — which would benefit equally those who stay and those who go — is to lower the school-leaving age to 14 for all who achieve some minimum national standard. This would solve the problem of the ineducable 15-year old, while at the same time giving the just about still educable 14-year old some realistic and attainable goal to motivate him. Schools would be spared the task of coping with the most difficult of their pupils, who could move on to apprenticeship and real work, and so acquire the maturity that is postponed by their unwillingly extended childhood.

This proposal will, of course, be objected to by various interested parties on a number of grounds. First, and most honourably, it will be said that in allowing 15- and 16-year olds to leave school we are depriving them of the opportunities to learn. Some, indeed, who might profit from being forced to stay on will miss out. But there is no reason why they should miss out altogether. They could be given vouchers or credits to take up education again when they are older and more prepared for it. And there is surely a strong ethical argument against forcing one's own vision of the good life (in this case education) on people who do not want it. Surely by the age of 14 most pupils should be able to read, write, spell, calculate and have enough general and scientific knowledge to find their way around the world. (The fact that many do not achieve this by the age of 16 reflects more on the education they are given, and the spirit in which they are given it, than on the intrinsic impossibility of the thing.)

A second argument against lowering the school-leaving age would be that the economy needs an educated and trained workforce. Claims of this sort have achieved the status of folk-wisdom among politicians and educators, but they need careful examination. There seems in fact to be no general correlation between educational achievement and economic success (and even less between length of education and economic success). While it is probably true that some very highly educated or trained people are needed in a modern economy (say 20% of the population), it is not so clear that the average standard of education needs to be particularly high for economic growth. The growth of technological knowledge — not necessarily widely shared in a society — and improved resource allocation seem far more relevant to economic growth than any growth in education. The latter, indeed, often follows rather than precedes the former. So economic arguments in favour of extending compulsory education need to be treated with caution.

A final argument in favour of maintaining compulsory education until the age of 16 is that the alternative will increase the numbers of young unemployed. But if the rationale for school is simply to keep young people off the streets, we should stop pretending that the main point of education is to benefit those who receive it. One wonders, indeed, what the benefit is to someone of 15 or 16 who is kept at school against his will and achieves nothing other than, say, a low-grade GCSE in integrated humanities (and, of course, many do not achieve even that). There is, in fact, no good reason to force unwilling pupils to stay at school once they have achieved an agreed minimum standard in English, Mathematics and Science.

d)   The Inspectorate

In a devolved education system, there will still be a role for school inspectors, a more significant role, indeed, than the current one in which they simply enforce an orthodoxy on the whole system. In the new system, just as in the old, the public in general and parents in particular will still require assurance of quality in education. Schools should therefore seek seals of approval from inspecting bodies which are genuinely impartial and independent, rather as at the moment independent preparatory schools have to be vetted before being allowed to join the association of independent preparatory schools, IPAS.

Qualified teachers and academics, including current inspectors, should be allowed to set themselves up as inspecting bodies. In a situation in which schools will have to compete for pupils in order to stay alive, schools will find it advantageous to possess and publish good reports from well-regarded boards of inspectors, just as in the old system it was advantageous for schools and pupils to pass examinations set by boards known to be rigorous (and will become so again under the examining system proposed here). Indeed, the inspecting companies might finance themselves in part by publishing consumer guides to schools, so as to enable parents to consider informed and objective comments on the strengths and aims of particular schools.

In their turn, those inspecting companies whose seal of approval the public came to trust would flourish. In this way, a new and healthy symbiosis would grow between schools and inspectors, to replace the old and corrupt one in which the inspectors and educational administrators were mutually supporting beneficiaries of the same state system. Not the smallest benefit of the new system would be the prospect of inspectors actually criticising fashionable trends in education, rather than falling over backwards to endorse them, and then blaming others lower down when things go wrong.

e)   Teacher Training

Schools should be allowed to induct would-be teachers with sufficient subject knowledge into the teaching profession, irrespective of whether they have been to a college or a department of education. After two years successful and supervised work within a school, probationary teachers should be accorded qualified teacher status. Some of the £300 million per annum which goes to colleges and departments of education for initial teacher training should be made available to schools which are willing and able to carry out teacher initiation programmes within their walls. In this way teachers could qualify through direct practical experience and without having to undertake theoretical courses of dubious or negative educational value. University graduates might well find this an attractive way into teaching. Apart from anything else, they would be paid while training. And many schools would welcome the opportunity to employ and train people like Mrs Garfield, who are currently either unable to enter the teaching profession or compelled to hide their real views in order to do so.

f)   **Censorship**

The dissolution of the monolithic and Stalinist system of education which we have in this country would mean that people with differing views could happily work in education. Schools of different sorts and with different characters would arise, and no doubt attract different sorts of pupils and different sorts of staff. A teacher who felt unhappy in one kind of school would not be faced with the difficult decision so many teachers are faced with today, either to conform to what he does not like or leave the profession altogether. He might well be able to find a school with whose practice he was more in sympathy. A freeing of the system would be of particular benefit to teachers whose views would currently be condemned as negative and old-fashioned. For there is in the country as a whole, I believe, a considerable demand for a more authoritarian type of education than the child-centered egalitarian style currently favoured. At any rate, educational traditionalists would be able to compete fairly with educational progressives, and the public rather than biased professionals would decide the outcome.

Conclusion

Our present crisis in education forces us to reflect on the meaning of democracy, and on whether institutions claiming and promoting authority can flourish within a democracy. On one interpretation of democracy they cannot: that which understands democracy as the promotion of egalitarian, anti-élitist values. But education cannot be egalitarian. It has to claim authority, and to recognise, promote and defer to élites. Our state system, subject to bureaucrats and ideologies, is incapable of doing this. Yet, in multiple ways, it fails all our children. Even by its own misguided standards, 30% of all teaching is poor or very poor. The best hope for education in this country and hence for our democracy too, is to remove education from the hands of government, and to give true authority the chance to flourish once more in the realms of learning and culture. A democracy which could give birth to the achievements of ancient Athens must be our aim.

Appendix: Education and Ancient Athens

In describing the threats to true education from the followers of John Dewey, I identified the 'Socratic spirit' as potentially destructive of the reverence for what one is studying. But, in *The Republic*, it is Socrates himself who is represented as describing the deleterious effects of the democratic spirit. There is a certain paradox here, because (in the view of Aristophanes and Nietzsche at least) Plato's Socrates was not the historical Socrates. Indeed, in their view it was precisely Socrates who, in conjunction with Euripides, did most to sap the aristocratic spirit which the best and most noble in ancient Athens expressed. For Nietzsche, Socrates was the ugly, snub-nosed little man, who was the revenge of the cowardly and litigious Thersites on the Achaean heroes. Socrates, with his quibbling, his cleverness and his endless and fruitless search for definition, destroyed the confidence of the best in what was best, and at the same time gave the common man, the man of the market place, the idea that he was the equal of Agammennon, Achilles and Odysseus.

> They sit at the feet of Socrates
> Till they can't distinguish the wood from the trees
> And tragedy goes to pot;
> They don't care whether their plays are art
> But only whether the words are smart
> They waste our time with quibbles and quarrels
> Destroying our patience as well as our morals
> And teaching us all to talk rot

(Aristophanes, *The Frogs,* Penguin translation lines 1491-9)

And Euripides:

Think of all the harm he has done. Hasn't he shown us pimps and profligates, women giving birth in temples and sleeping with their brothers and saying that life is not life? Isn't that why the city is so full of lawyers' clerks and scrounging mountebanks, swindling the community right and left? And not a decent athlete left in the whole city, they're all out of training.

(*The Frogs*, lines 1080-6)

Euripides would say — what Aristophanes represented him as saying — that what he did was to teach his audience to use its brains and that the public has learned from him how to think. But there is thinking and thinking, and 'teaching people to use their brains' can all too easily result in a kind of ignorant and self-satisfied scepticism, an impermeable discontent with whatever is, with whatever one has not chosen for oneself and whatever one cannot immediately see the reason for. Unfortunately we have in our time no Aeschylus or Aristophanes to put such shallow thinkers in their place:

Look how you have encouraged people to babble and prate. The wrestling schools are empty, and where have all the young men gone? Off to those infamous establishments (institutions of 'student-centred' learning?) where they practice the art of debating, and that isn't all they practice there either ...

(*The Frogs*, line 1074-8)

I have no doubt that the portrait painted of Socrates in *The Frogs* and even more that in *The Birth of Tragedy* are partial and biased. Indeed, one could just as well argue (as I F Stone did in *The Trial of Socrates*) that it was Socrates's hostility to democracy and his closeness to the oligarchs of 411 BC (to say nothing of his friendship with Alcibiades) that formed the background to his eventual condemnation at the hands of the Athenian democracy.

Socrates, indeed, was no egalitarian and would not have subscribed to the doctrines of Dewey's *Democracy and Education*. He would never have followed Dewey in seeing the role of the teacher as being that of leader of group activities. Nevertheless, there is something in the Socratic spirit which is dangerous to true education; this is what Aristophanes and Nietzsche had put their finger on. And it may explain why in the *Republic* Plato found it necessary to have his Socrates — another Socrates — basing a system of education on music and gymnastic. I conjecture that we might see the *Republic* as an attempt, perhaps 20 or more years after the event, to rebut the portrait of Socrates with which Aristophanes presents us in *The Frogs* and *The Clouds,* a portrait in which there is more than a grain of truth.

According to the *Republic* in the early stages of education, the spirit of criticism and pupil chatter is to be firmly discouraged. In the first place, the child will be exposed to myths of various sorts in which goodness will be represented and made attractive. Plato is, of course, notorious for his insistence on censoring the poets, not just the likes of Euripides and the new comedians, but Homer himself. Gods and heroes are not to be shown indulging in dalliance, deceit and other vices. In my opinion it would be a considerable step forward if our children were to learn anything about classical gods and heroes, even about their vices. It is also, as I know from experience, perfectly possible for quite young children to be excited by stories such as the Odyssey, the Labours of Hercules, the Trojan War and even by some of Ovid's *Metamorphoses.* In hearing these things they will begin to learn about the roots of our culture, and, despite what Plato says, they will learn a lot of truth about morality and the human condition: they will learn about the fragility and frequent injustice of life, about the ineluctability of fate, about the need for work and for steadfastness, about the unity of man and nature, about the beauty of home and hearth, about companionship and hospitality, and much else besides. They will also learn that there are gods and heroes, that not all men are equal and that no one is wholly perfectible, and all this will prepare in them an attitude of respect towards their superiors. It will, among other things, prepare them for a properly serious and reverential attitude to academic study.

So, without sharing Plato's censoriousness about the classics, his proposals for teaching young children about gods and heroes can be endorsed on several grounds. So, too, can what he says about music. I have no doubt that there is a strong connection between the indiscipline of young people and the music they favour, with its rhythmic barbarity, its hedonistic and rebellious messages, and its sentimental assumption that there are easy and instant solutions to every problem, personal, social and political. Even though the tastes of the young cannot be effectively censored in a free society, the young can be given an education which might direct their preferences on sounder lines:

> Then, Glaucon, is not musical education of paramount importance, because rhythm and harmony enter most powerfully into the innermost part of the soul and lay forcible hands upon it, bearing grace with him who is rightly trained, and him who is not, the reverse? Is it not a further reason that he who has been rightly trained in music would be quick to observe all works of art that were defective or ugly, and all natural objects that failed in beauty? They would displease him, and rightly, but beautiful things he would praise, and receiving them with joy into his soul, would be nourished by them, and become noble and good. Ugly things he would rightly condemn, and that even in his youth before he was capable of reason; but when reason comes he would welcome her as one who knows, with whom his training has made him familiar.

That is from Plato's *Republic* (section 401), but we find a strikingly similar thought in Aristotle's *Politics*. Music has indeed 'a power of forming the character, and should therefore be introduced into the education of the young', (*Pol.* 13 40b 10), educated in it, Aristotle would say, to recognise the superiority of the Dorian mode over the Phrygian, which puts man into a frenzy of excitement. Plato and Aristotle would both have been appalled by electronic pop music, and even more by the thought that its barbaric tones and rhythms should be given a place in institutions devoted to the upbringing of the young, as our School Inspectorate demands, and as the GCSE music syllabus encourages.

It is the fundamental insight of Plato's and Aristotle's thinking on education that reason in the correct sense follows a proper training in attitude and morality. By reason, of course, they do not mean the babbling and prating condemned by Aristophanes, and of which Aristophanes found Socrates guilty. They mean rather what I earlier referred to as right reason or reasonableness. Aristotle is particularly clear about the relationship of wisdom to cleverness:

> There is a faculty called cleverness; and this is such as to be able to do the things that tend towards the mark we have set before ourselves, and to hit it. Now if the mark be noble, the cleverness is laudable, but if the mark be bad, the cleverness is mere smartness ... for wickedness perverts us and causes us to be deceived about the starting points of action. Therefore it is evident that it is impossible to be practically wise without being good.

That is to say, we can be clever and 'reason' in a way which leads us away from what is good and worthwhile. (This, of course, is Aristophanes' complaint about Socrates and Euripides.) According to Aristotle and Plato, virtue — the disposition to choose and value what is good — is a matter of acquiring the right habits when young:

> it makes no small difference, then, whether we form habits of one kind or of another from our very youth: it makes a very great difference, or rather *all* the difference.

(*Nic. Eth.*, 1103b 24-5)

It is true that in discussing practical wisdom, Aristotle is principally concerned with the acquisition of good morals in public and private life. But it is not difficult to extend what he has to say to other areas of education, intellectual and cultural, as I have done in the body of this pamphlet. We then see education first and foremost as a matter of initiation into pre-existing forms of thought and expression, and of the acquisition of appropriate habits and dispositions.

Intellectual and moral education, then, must start with a

training in the appropriate habits and virtues, partly because a child's reasoning powers develop slower and later than his passions and his body. Aristotle draws another interesting consequence from this fact:

> As the body comes into being earlier than the soul, so also the unreasoning part is prior to that which possesses reason. This is shown by the fact that, while passion and will as well as desire are to be found in children even right from birth, reasoning and intelligence come into their possession as they grow older. Therefore the care of the body must begin before the care of the soul ... but the body's training for the sake of the soul.

> (*Politics*, 1334b 20-28)

Should education include 'the care of the body'? Are Aristotle (and Plato) right in seeing a properly motivated gymnastic as an essential part of a proper education? In face of Aristophanic complaints about the dire effects of the emptying of the wrestling schools, it is tempting to suppose that they are. While a lack of gymnastic may not be the biggest failure in our educational system at present, an obsessive concern with children's health and safety might be symptomatic of the malaise which confronts us. In the classical conception, part of the point of gymnastic was to instil a certain steel and courage and self-forgetfulness in children, and to allow those who could excel in a particular area to do so. Morally it was an aspect of that overcoming of self which is part of true education. It seems to me that physical education does have an important role to play in instilling the habits of self-discipline and steadfastness which are crucial to the upbringing of the young. So, as with music, the Greeks were right to include gymnastic as a vital part of the curriculum.

My conclusion, then, is that we have much to learn about education from Aristophanes, Plato and Aristotle. Apart from the stress on music and gymnastic, we would do well to learn from them that genuinely humane education can proceed only on the assumption that the learners need first and foremost to acquire certain habits of mind and behaviour, and to submit themselves to the judgments of authorities, without forever attempting to criticise 'received notions and methodologies'. Plato and Aristotle would have been well aware that the 'criticism of established forms' is often only the uncritical parroting of other received ideas, and never more so than when the context of the criticism is an ostensibly contentless and child-centred curriculum.

My arguments in this Appendix, and in the pamphlet generally, are not *per se* undemocratic. It is worth remembering that the audience for whom Aeschylus wrote was a democracy just as much as that for which Euripides wrote. Because the common man did not strut upon Aeschylus's stage, it does not mean that the visions conjured up by the playwright were not visions which encapsulated the hopes, fears and aspirations of the common man. Democratic Athens honoured Aeschylus during his lifetime and continued to honour his plays and to reward those who produced them after his death. The task is to create a democracy in which real differences of quality and of intellect are recognised, and in which the best can flourish. This is not just a political issue; it is precisely the main concern of education in our day.